WILDERNESS WINS

What Looks Like Defeat
Is Often Divine Preparation

Based on Mark 1:9–13

DR. STUART A. MONCRIEFFE

Wilderness Wins: What Looks Like Defeat is Often Divine Protection

ISBN: 979-8-9883287-7-3

www.globalscribespublications.com

For every soul in the wilderness—
you are not lost. You are being prepared.

Dedication

To my beloved wife,
Apostle Nurita Moncrieffe,

Thank you for walking beside me through every season — through the mountaintops and the wilderness. Your strength, your prayers, and your faithfulness to God have been a covering and a blessing in ways words cannot fully express.

You have stood firm when things were uncertain, believed when it was difficult, and remained faithful through it all. This work carries the imprint of your support, your love, and your sacrifice.

I honor you, I celebrate you, and I thank God for you.

Preface

Every person who has ever walked with God has, at some point, found themselves in a wilderness. Not a wilderness of their own making — though those exist too — but a wilderness of divine design. A season stripped of comfort, stripped of noise, stripped of the familiar, where the only company seems to be silence and pressure.

This book grows out of a simple but transformative conviction: the wilderness is not where God abandons you. It is where God prepares you.

In Mark 1:9–13, we encounter Jesus in just such a moment. Fresh from the waters of baptism, affirmed by the voice of the Father, anointed by the Spirit — and then immediately driven into the wilderness. Forty days of temptation. Wild beasts. Exposure. And yet, when He emerges, He steps into the fullness of His public ministry with authority, clarity, and power.

What if that is the pattern for us as well?

What if the season you are desperately trying to escape is the very season God is using to establish what cannot be shaken in you?

These pages are for the believer under pressure. For the one who has heard God clearly but finds life harder than expected. For the one who is fighting battles in hidden places, whose victories no one will applaud, whose endurance no one will celebrate — not yet.

The wilderness is not your end. It is your school. And the One who walked it before you is with you still.

CONTENTS

INTRODUCTION

The Place Nobody Wants

Have you ever experienced a season in life when everything felt stripped down?

The crowd gets quiet. The comfort gets removed. The support seems limited. The road gets rough. The air gets dry. The place becomes unfamiliar.

That is what the Bible calls the wilderness.

No one volunteers for the wilderness. No one prays, "Lord, give me a season of dryness, difficulty, and exposure." Yet the wilderness is one of the most consistent themes in the story of God's people. Abraham waited. Moses fled. Elijah collapsed. David hid. And Jesus — the Son of God Himself — was driven into the wilderness immediately after His baptism.

This tells us something important: the wilderness is not a sign that something has gone wrong. For the people of

God, it is often a sign that something is being made right — something deep, something permanent, something that cannot be built any other way.

The wilderness is not where you are abandoned.

It is where you are prepared.

The wilderness is not only a place of testing — it is also a place of proving. It is not only where the enemy speaks — it is where God settles who you are. It is not only where you feel weak — it is where heaven demonstrates that grace is stronger than pressure.

You are not losing in the wilderness. You are learning how to win there.

This book walks through the brief but powerful account of Mark 1:9–13 — Jesus' baptism and wilderness experience — and unpacks six truths that will shift how you see every difficult season you face. My prayer is that by the time you turn the final page, you will not merely endure the wilderness. You will understand it, embrace it, and emerge from it ready.

CHAPTER ONE

The Wilderness Often Comes After a Divine Confirmation

"And immediately the Spirit
drove Him into the wilderness."
– Mark 1:12

Mark moves with remarkable speed. In just a few verses, Jesus is baptized, the heavens open, the Spirit descends like a dove, and the Father speaks: "You are My beloved Son, in whom I am well pleased."

Then, immediately, He is driven into the wilderness.

The wilderness came after affirmation.

This sequence should reframe how you interpret hardship. Many people assume that if God has spoken over them, the next season will be smooth. If God confirmed the vision, the path forward should be clear. If the Spirit descended at your baptism, your wilderness days should be finished.

But that is not what the Scriptures show us.

Often, after God confirms you, life confronts you. After the promise comes the pressure. After the word comes the warfare. After the anointing comes the attack.

The Shock of Sudden Transition

One of the most overlooked aspects of this moment is not just that the wilderness came after affirmation, but how quickly it came. There was no pause between the voice of the Father and the pressure of the wilderness. No transition period. No gradual easing into difficulty. One moment Jesus is standing in divine affirmation, and the next He is stepping into divine testing. This sudden shift can be deeply unsettling for believers because we often expect that when God speaks, there will be time to enjoy, celebrate, or settle into what was said. But sometimes, the very next step after confirmation is confrontation. Not because something has gone wrong, but because something has begun. God does not always give you time to become comfortable with what He has spoken before

He begins to develop you through it. The speed of the transition is intentional. It prevents you from building your confidence on the moment instead of on God. It teaches you early that your stability cannot come from experiences, even spiritual ones, but from a deeper anchoring in Him.

The Enemy Attacks What Heaven Has Declared

Jesus had just heard, "You are My beloved Son." And what was the focus of Satan's temptation in the wilderness? His sonship. His identity.

The enemy always attacks what heaven has already declared.

Some people believe the battle they are in is evidence they have missed God. But the truth may be the opposite. The battle may be happening precisely because God has marked you. The pressure may be proof that your next season carries weight. Hell does not waste its energy on empty people. The enemy fights where destiny is present.

Do not panic because life grew harder after God spoke. Do not assume the wilderness means the word failed. The wilderness is often where the word gets rooted deeply in you.

You heard God in the water. Now you must remember Him in the wilderness.

When the Environment Does Not Match the Word

There is a unique discomfort that comes when what God has spoken over your life does not seem to match the environment you find yourself in. You carry a word that speaks of purpose, identity, and calling, yet you are surrounded by conditions that feel restrictive, dry, or even contrary. This disconnect can create internal tension if it is not understood correctly. But the wilderness is often the place where God separates what He said from what you see, so that your faith is not dependent on visible alignment. If every environment matched the word immediately, you would never develop the ability to believe beyond what is in front of you. The wilderness trains your perception. It teaches you how to hold truth in one hand while facing contradiction in the other without losing your footing. It develops a steadiness that is not shaken by inconsistency between promise and present reality. In this way, the wilderness becomes a place where your trust matures beyond circumstances and becomes anchored in the character of God.

Heaven Spoke First

Here is a sequence worth anchoring in your heart:

The Father's voice came before the devil's voice.
Identity was established before temptation arrived.
Heaven spoke first.

That means what God said about you is greater than what the wilderness says about you.

You may be in a dry season, but you are still beloved.
You may be in a hard season, but you are still chosen.
You may be in a lonely season, but you are still called.

Pressure cannot cancel promise.

Carrying the Echo of God's Voice

When God speaks, His word does not expire when the moment ends. It continues beyond the experience, and in the wilderness, it becomes something you must learn to carry without constant reinforcement. You are no longer standing in the moment where the voice was heard; you are standing in a place where it must be remembered. This requires intentionality. You must learn to carry what was spoken, to revisit it, to rehearse it, and to allow it to shape your responses in a season where clarity may not always be present. The wilderness teaches you how to steward what you have already received. It trains you to value the word enough to hold onto it when there is no external affirmation. And in doing so, it deepens your relationship with God, not only as One who speaks, but as One whose word is strong enough to sustain you even in silence.

CHAPTER TWO

If the Spirit Led You There, Grace Will Keep You There

"And He was there in the wilderness forty days, tempted by Satan."
— Mark 1:13

Mark does not say Jesus wandered into the wilderness. He says Jesus was driven there. The word suggests compulsion, urgency, intentionality. This was not an accident.

Jesus was not lost. He was led. He was not outside of divine order. He was in the center of it.

This distinction is critical.

There are wilderness seasons we create through disobedience. When we walk away from God, when we make choices that lead us into barren places, those wildernesses are the consequences of our own turning.

But there are also wilderness seasons that God permits by design — seasons the Spirit leads us into because something essential must be formed there that could not be formed anywhere else.

The Intentionality of God in Uncomfortable Places

It is important to understand that when God leads you into a wilderness, He is not experimenting with your life. There is nothing random about the process, and there is nothing careless about the placement. Every uncomfortable season carries intention. God knows exactly what He is addressing, what He is removing, and what He is establishing within you. The discomfort is not evidence of absence; it is often evidence of precision. God is not broadly working on your life; He is specifically working on areas that must be strengthened for where you are going. This is why wilderness seasons often feel targeted. The pressure seems to touch specific thoughts, habits, and responses. That is not coincidence; that is design. When you understand that God is intentional, it changes how you interpret the season. You move from asking why this is happening to recognizing that God is working with purpose even in places that feel unclear.

The Wilderness Strips Away the Props

The wilderness is uncomfortable because it removes the things we lean on that are not God.

In comfortable seasons, we can confuse our titles with our anointing. We can mistake applause for affirmation. We can lean on relationships and routines and familiar structures — and never discover whether our faith is truly rooted in God Himself or in the conditions that surround us.

The wilderness removes all of that. And what remains reveals what has truly been built in you.

Some of us want public victory with private weakness. But God says, "Before I display you, I will develop you. Before I send you out, I will settle you within."

What the Wilderness Removes That You Didn't Notice

One of the hidden mercies of the wilderness is that it removes things you may not have realized were shaping you. In more stable seasons, it is easy to carry subtle dependencies without recognizing their influence. You may rely on consistency, familiarity, or even the approval of others more than you realize. These things are not always wrong, but they can quietly become substitutes for deeper dependence on God. The wilderness interrupts that. It removes excess. It breaks patterns. It exposes what has been operating beneath the surface. This is not to condemn you, but to free you. Because what remains hidden can continue to influence you without your awareness. In the wilderness, God brings clarity. He allows you to see what was previously overlooked so that you can release what is unnecessary and become strengthened in what truly matters.

Not Left — Still Present

If the Spirit led Jesus into the wilderness, then being in a hard place does not automatically mean you are out of

God's will. Sometimes you are precisely where heaven intended for you to be.

And here is the comfort: if the Spirit led you in, the Spirit will sustain you through.

You may not like the place, but God has not left the place. You may not understand the season, but God is still Lord over the season.
You may not know how long the wilderness is, but you can know who is with you in it.

Staying When Leaving Feels Easier

There are moments in a wilderness season when the greatest temptation is not failure, but escape. The desire to find relief can become stronger as the pressure continues and the timeline remains uncertain. It can feel easier to step away, to search for comfort, or to move ahead of God simply to ease the tension. But not every exit is obedience. Sometimes leaving too soon means stepping out before the work is complete. The wilderness requires a different kind of strength — not the strength to overcome externally, but the strength to remain internally aligned when everything in you desires relief.

Staying does not mean passivity; it means commitment to what God is doing. It means trusting that completion matters more than comfort. When you learn to remain until God releases you, you come out not only having endured the season, but having been fully shaped by it.

Grace for Where You Are, Not Just Where You're Going

Grace is often understood as the power that brings breakthrough, but in the wilderness, grace reveals itself as the power that sustains. It meets you where you are, not just where you are going. It strengthens you in the middle of uncertainty, steadies you in the middle of pressure, and keeps you anchored when clarity feels distant. This kind of grace does not always change your environment immediately, but it changes your capacity within it. It allows you to continue, to remain, and to stay aligned even when the season is difficult. And often, it is in this kind of grace that you discover a deeper dimension of God's faithfulness — not just as One who delivers, but as One who sustains.

CHAPTER THREE

The Wilderness Is Where Identity Is Tested — and Where Identity Is Proven

"You are My beloved
Son, in whom I am well pleased."
— Mark 1:11

Jesus is tempted by Satan. Though Mark is brief, the Gospel accounts show us that the temptation centered on the same thing the Father had just spoken over Him: His sonship. His identity. His relationship to God.

The wilderness becomes the courtroom of identity. The enemy challenges what God has declared.

That is still how he works.

Identity Under Interrogation

In the wilderness, identity is not casually questioned; it is aggressively interrogated. The pressure is not random, and the questions are not harmless. They are designed to wear down your certainty, to create internal instability, and to make you reconsider what God has already made clear. This is why the wilderness can feel so intense. It is not merely external pressure; it is internal confrontation. You are not just dealing with what is happening around you, but with what is being suggested within you. The enemy understands that if he can weaken your confidence in who you are, he can influence how you respond. Because identity governs behavior. If identity becomes unstable, decisions become compromised. But if identity remains settled, even under pressure, your responses will remain aligned with what God has already established.

The Enemy Loves the Word "If"

Temptation rarely attacks the obvious. It attacks the settled. The voice in the wilderness whispers:

"If you were really called..."
"If you were really anointed..."
"If God was really with you..."
"If you were really chosen, why is it this hard?"

Heaven said, "You are." Hell says, "If..."

That is how temptation works. It tries to pull you from divine certainty into human insecurity. It tries to get you to perform for what you already possess. It tries to make you prove by flesh what has already been established by God.

Jesus wins because He refuses to let the wilderness redefine Him.

The Pressure to Perform

One of the most subtle traps in the wilderness is the pressure to perform in order to feel secure. When identity feels challenged, there is a natural pull to do something that will validate who you are. To prove your calling. To demonstrate your worth. To confirm that God is truly with you. But this is where many people fall into unnecessary striving. The moment you begin to perform for what God has already declared, you step out of rest and into effort. The wilderness exposes this tendency. It reveals how quickly we can move from identity to performance when we feel uncertain. But true identity does not need to be proven; it needs to be believed. Jesus did not respond to temptation by trying to prove He was the Son. He responded from the confidence that He already was. And in the same way, the wilderness teaches you to live from what has been established, not to strive for what has already been given.

You Do Not Have to Earn What Grace Already Named

You do not have to compromise to confirm your calling. You do not have to bow to pressure to prove you belong to God.

The wilderness will ask its questions:

"Who are you when nobody is clapping?"
"Who are you when the door is shut?"
"Who are you when the answer is delayed?"
"Who are you when you are still waiting?"

Your answer: *"I am who God said I am — whether I feel it or not."*

Identity Beyond Feeling

One of the most important developments in the wilderness is learning to separate identity from emotion. Feelings are real, but they are not always reliable indicators of truth. There will be moments when you do not feel chosen, do not feel strong, and do not feel certain. The wilderness has a way of amplifying those emotional fluctuations. But identity cannot be built on how you feel in a moment; it must be grounded in what God has declared over you. This is where maturity is formed. You learn to stand in truth even when your emotions are unsettled. You learn to respond based on what has been established, not what is being felt. And over time, your identity becomes less reactive and more rooted. It is no longer shaken by every change in circumstance or emotion. It becomes steady, anchored, and secure.

The Quiet Proving of Identity

The wilderness does not just test identity; it quietly proves it. Not through public recognition or visible affirmation, but through consistent, internal alignment. Every time you choose not to compromise, every time you refuse to agree with doubt, every time you hold on to what God said without external confirmation, something is being proven within you. You are not becoming something new; you are demonstrating what has already been established. This kind of proving is not loud, but it is powerful. It does not draw attention, but it builds strength. And when the season shifts, you will not need to wonder who you are. You will know, because it has been tested, refined, and proven in a place where nothing external could sustain it.

CHAPTER FOUR

The Enemy Can Test You, But He Cannot Own You

"He was with the wild beasts."
– Mark 1:13

Mark does not sanitize the wilderness. He lets us feel it. Wild beasts. Forty days. Temptation. This is not a soft, romantic retreat. It is dangerous. It is hard. It is exposed.

But notice what is missing: nowhere does the text suggest that Satan ruled Jesus there. Satan tempted Him. But he did not triumph over Him.

The enemy may be touching your season, but he does not own your future. He may be fighting your mind, but he does not own your identity. He may be resisting your progress, but he does not control your purpose.

The Limits of the Enemy

It is important to understand that the enemy operates within limits. His presence does not equal authority, and his activity does not mean control. He can suggest, he can pressure, and he can attempt to influence, but he cannot override what God has established. The wilderness may feel intense, but it is not ungoverned. God has not stepped off the throne simply because the environment feels hostile. There is a boundary to what the enemy can do, and there is a line he cannot cross. Recognizing this changes how you respond. Instead of reacting out of fear, you begin to stand with awareness. You realize that while the enemy may be active, he is not in charge. And that understanding allows you to remain steady even when the pressure feels strong.

Biblical Victory Looks Different Than We Expect

Sometimes believers think victory means the absence of a fight. But biblical victory often looks different: you came through the fight with your obedience intact. With your worship intact. With your faith intact. With your integrity intact.

You can be under pressure and still be under God. You can be attacked and still be anointed. You can be in the wilderness and still be in victory.

The presence of warfare is not proof of the absence of God.

Remaining Intact Under Pressure

The true evidence of victory is not always seen in what has changed around you, but in what has been preserved within you. The wilderness applies pressure, but pressure does not have to produce damage. It can instead reveal stability. When you come through a difficult season still aligned, still committed, and still anchored, something significant has taken place. You have demonstrated that your foundation is not easily shaken. Many people measure victory by outward outcomes, but God often measures it by inward consistency. Can you remain the same in character when the environment shifts? Can you stay grounded when circumstances fluctuate? This is the kind of strength that is formed in the wilderness. It is not loud, but it is durable. It is not always visible, but it is deeply established.

Anyone can shout on the mountain. But can you still trust Him in the wilderness? Anyone can worship in abundance. But can you still bless Him in scarcity? Anyone can testify after the breakthrough. But can you stand while the answer is still forming?

That is wilderness winning.

Authority Without Visibility

One of the most overlooked realities of the wilderness is that authority can be developed without visibility. You may not be seen, recognized, or affirmed during this season, but something is still being established within you. Authority is not only revealed in public; it is formed in private. It is shaped in moments where no one is watching, where there is no external validation, and where your choices are made purely out of conviction. The wilderness becomes the place where your responses carry weight, even if no one else sees them. Every decision to remain aligned, every moment you refuse to give in to pressure, contributes to a level of authority that cannot be manufactured later. When the time comes for you to step forward, what was developed in hidden places will support you in visible ones.

You Are Not at the Mercy of the Moment

The wilderness can create the illusion that you are at the mercy of your circumstances, but that is not the truth. While you may not control the environment, you are not powerless within it. You still have the ability to choose your response, to guard your posture, and to remain aligned with God. This is where strength is exercised. The enemy may attempt to shape the situation, but he does not get to determine your outcome. You are not being carried by the moment; you are being shaped within it. And as you continue to respond with faithfulness, something greater than the pressure is being formed in you. You are not simply surviving the wilderness; you are establishing a level of stability that will carry you beyond it.

CHAPTER FIVE

God Will Send Help in the Place of Pressure

"And the angels ministered to Him."
– Mark 1:13

After everything Mark has described — the temptation, the wild beasts, the forty days — he adds this one quiet, extraordinary line: the angels ministered to Him.

Heaven did not stop watching because the environment got rough. Divine assistance came into a difficult place.

The wilderness is not empty. It may look barren, but it is not abandoned. It may feel silent, but it is not unsupported.

Help Does Not Always Arrive Loudly

One of the most important things to understand about divine help is that it does not always arrive in dramatic or obvious ways. Sometimes we expect help to come with visible interruption, immediate change, or unmistakable signs. But often, God's ministry is quiet, subtle, and deeply personal. It meets you in ways that others may not see or fully understand. It may not shift the entire environment at once, but it will strengthen you within it. If you are only looking for help in loud expressions, you may miss the ways God is already sustaining you. The ability to keep going, the peace that settles your thoughts, the strength that rises when you feel weak — these are not small things. They are evidence that God is present and actively ministering, even in ways that are not always visible.

The Many Forms of Divine Ministry

God knows how to send ministry into desolate places. It does not always look the same.

Sometimes He sends angelic help — unseen but unmistakable.

Sometimes He sends strength you cannot explain.
Sometimes He sends a word that arrives at exactly the right moment.
Sometimes He sends peace in the middle of panic.
Sometimes He sends a song in the night.
Sometimes He sends unexpected provision.
Sometimes He sends a praying friend at just the right moment.
Sometimes He sends holy endurance — the quiet ability to keep going.

But one way or another, God ministers to His people in the wilderness.

God Knows What You Need — Not Just What You Want

God's ministry is not random; it is precise. He does not simply respond to what you are asking for; He responds to what you actually need. There are times when you may desire immediate relief, but God provides sustaining strength instead. There are moments when you want answers, but He gives you peace. There are seasons when you ask for change, but He gives you endurance. This does not mean He has ignored you; it means He is responding with wisdom. God understands what will carry you through the season, not just what will make you feel better in the moment. His help is not always shaped by your expectation; it is shaped by His understanding. And because of that, His ministry is always effective, even when it looks different than what you anticipated.

The wilderness may strip away your illusion of control. But it will introduce you to the faithfulness of God in a way that nothing else can.

Faithfulness Experienced, Not Just Believed

There is a difference between believing that God is faithful and experiencing His faithfulness. In easier seasons, faithfulness can remain a concept, something you agree with but have not deeply encountered. But in the wilderness, it becomes personal. You begin to recognize that God is not only faithful in theory, but faithful in practice. He meets you consistently, even when circumstances are inconsistent. He sustains you repeatedly, even when the pressure does not immediately lift. Over time, your confidence in God shifts from something you were taught to something you have lived.

And that kind of confidence cannot be easily shaken, because it has been formed through experience.

You will come out of this season with something you could not have received in comfort: testimony.

"He kept me."
"He sustained me."
"He covered me."
"He strengthened me."
"He did not let me break."

Testimony That Is Built, Not Borrowed

The testimony that comes out of the wilderness is different because it is built, not borrowed. It is not something you heard from someone else or admired from a distance. It is something you have lived through personally. It carries weight because it was formed in real pressure, real uncertainty, and real dependence on God. When you speak from that place, it is not just words; it is evidence. It reflects a relationship with God that has been tested and proven through experience. And that testimony does more than encourage others; it reminds you of what God has already done. It becomes a reference point for future seasons, a reminder that if He sustained you before, He will sustain you again.

CHAPTER SIX

Your Wilderness Is Preparation for Your Witness

"Now after John was put in prison,
Jesus came to Galilee, preaching the
gospel of the kingdom of God."
— Mark 1:14

Mark places Jesus' wilderness account directly before the beginning of His public ministry. The wilderness was not the end of the story. It was preparation for what came next.

Do not miss this. Victory in private precedes authority in public. Winning in hidden places prepares you for visible assignments. When you defeat the enemy in the wilderness, you do not come out empty. You come out sharpened.

The Transition From Hidden to Visible

There is a shift that takes place when a wilderness season comes to completion. It is not always announced, and it is not always dramatic, but it is real. What was once hidden begins to move toward visibility. What was once internal begins to find expression. This transition is not based on your desire to be seen; it is based on your readiness to be released. God does not move you forward simply because time has passed, but because something within you has been established. The wilderness is not measured only by duration, but by development. When the necessary work has been done, movement follows. And when it does, you step forward not as someone who is trying to become ready, but as someone who has already been prepared.

What the Wilderness Teaches You

The wilderness teaches you what classrooms and conferences cannot:

How to hear God without distraction.
How to resist the enemy without compromise.
How to endure pressure without collapsing.

How to trust heaven without visible evidence.
How to walk in authority without needing applause.

There are things you only learn in the wilderness. There are dimensions of God you only meet in the wilderness. There are battles you only win in the wilderness.

Formation Before Function

Before God uses you in a visible way, He forms you in a hidden place. This order is not accidental; it is essential. Function without formation leads to instability, but formation before function produces consistency. The wilderness becomes the place where your inner life is strengthened to support your outer assignment. What you carry publicly must be supported by what has been built privately. Without that foundation, success can become a strain instead of a stewardship. But when you have been properly formed, what you step into does not overwhelm you, because you have already been prepared for it in ways that others may not have seen. The wilderness ensures that what you carry is not just impressive, but sustainable.

When you come out, you do not just come out relieved. You come out ready.

Readiness Looks Different Than Expectation

Many people expect readiness to feel like confidence without pressure, clarity without questions, and strength without resistance. But readiness often looks different. It looks like steadiness, not perfection. It looks like alignment, not complete understanding. It looks like the ability to move forward even when everything is not fully clear. The wilderness prepares you for this kind of readiness. It teaches you how to function without needing everything to feel comfortable. It trains you to move with God even when the path is still unfolding. This is the kind of readiness that allows you to step into what God has for you without being dependent on ideal conditions.

Your Experience Becomes Your Voice

What you walk through in the wilderness does not stay there. It becomes part of how you speak, how you lead, and how you impact others. Your witness is not built from information alone; it is built from experience. The lessons you learned, the pressure you endured, and the ways God sustained you all become part of the authority you carry. When you speak, you are not speaking from theory; you are speaking from what you have lived. And that kind of voice carries weight. It reaches people differently because it is rooted in something real. The wilderness gives you more than endurance; it gives you substance. And that substance becomes part of your witness.

FINAL CHARGE

The Wilderness Did Not Come to Bury You

Jesus did not avoid the wilderness. He entered it full of the Spirit, stood in it with authority, and emerged from it prepared for ministry.

That is the invitation of this book: stop reading your wilderness only through the lens of pain. Start reading it through the lens of purpose.

The wilderness is where false dependencies die.
The wilderness is where identity gets anchored.
The wilderness is where the enemy gets resisted.
The wilderness is where heaven ministers.
The wilderness is where preparation happens.

And because Jesus won, you can win too.

You are not the first to stand in a hard place. Your Savior has already gone before you. He has already faced the adversary. He has already overcome. That means your wilderness does not have the final word.

Christ does!!

What You Thought Was Delay Was Development

There are seasons you may have interpreted as delay, times when it felt like progress had slowed or opportunities had paused. But what if those moments were not delay at all? What if they were development? The wilderness has a way of redefining time. It may not move at the pace you expect, but it moves with purpose. Every moment carries weight, even when it feels uneventful. God is not withholding from you; He is preparing you. And when you begin to see it that way, frustration begins to shift into understanding. You realize that nothing was wasted. Every difficult moment, every quiet season, every place of pressure contributed to who you have become. And because of that, you can step forward without regret, knowing that even what felt like delay was part of your preparation.

A Prayer for Every Reader in the Wilderness

Father, in the name of Jesus, I pray for every person who has held this book in a wilderness season. Let strength come now. Let clarity come now. Let healing come now.

Silence the voice of the enemy and amplify the voice of the Father. Send ministry into every barren place. Settle identity. Deepen obedience. Strengthen faith.

Let this be a season of overcomers. Let what looked like isolation become revelation. Let what felt like defeat become divine preparation.

Stabilize every wavering heart. Anchor every uncertain mind. Restore what has been drained and renew what has grown weary. Let peace guard them where pressure has tried to overwhelm them, and let Your presence become undeniable in the places that have felt silent.

Give them grace to remain, wisdom to discern, and courage to trust You even when they do not understand the process. Let no part of this season be wasted, but let it produce strength, clarity, and unshakable confidence in You.

In Jesus' name, Amen.

The wilderness did not come to bury you.

It came to build you.

And by the grace of God —

Wilderness Wins.

More from the Author

If this book has encouraged, strengthened, or challenged you in your walk with God, there are additional resources available to support your continued growth.

Explore more books by this author on Amazon, covering topics of spiritual growth, identity, deliverance, and walking in purpose.

Search by the author's name to discover more.

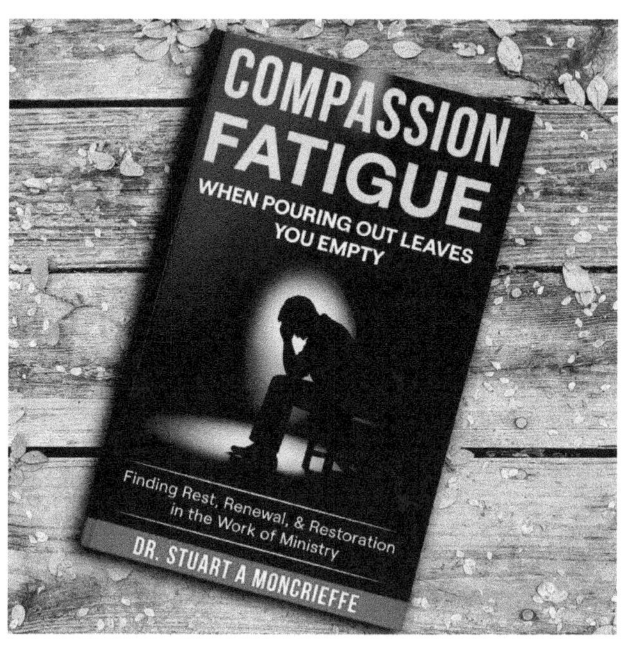
COMPASSION
FATIGUE
WHEN POURING OUT LEAVES
YOU EMPTY
Finding Rest, Renewal, & Restoration
in the Work of Ministry
DR. STUART A MONCRIEFFE

www.ingramcontent.com/pod-product-compliance
Lightning Source LLC
La Vergne TN
LVHW010546100826
845148LV00013B/2620
* 9 7 9 8 9 8 8 3 2 8 7 7 3 *